CELLO

2ND EDITION

THE BEST OF
The Beatles

ISBN 978-1-4234-1049-2

HAL•LEONARD®
CORPORATION
7777 W. BLUEMOUND RD. P.O. BOX 13819 MILWAUKEE. WI 53213

Visit Hal Leonard Online at
www.halleonard.com

CONTENTS

ALL MY LOVING

CELLO

Words and Music by JOHN LENNON
and PAUL McCARTNEY

ACROSS THE UNIVERSE

Cello

Words and Music by JOHN LENNON
and PAUL McCARTNEY

Slowly and smoothly

ALL YOU NEED IS LOVE

CELLO

Words and Music by JOHN LENNON
and PAUL McCARTNEY

Moderately

AND I LOVE HER

Cello

Words and Music by JOHN LENNON
and PAUL McCARTNEY

BACK IN THE U.S.S.R.

CELLO

Words and Music by JOHN LENNON
and PAUL McCARTNEY

THE BALLAD OF JOHN AND YOKO

CELLO

Words and Music by JOHN LENNON
and PAUL McCARTNEY

BECAUSE

CELLO

Words and Music by JOHN LENNON
and PAUL McCARTNEY

BIRTHDAY

CELLO

Words and Music by JOHN LENNON
and PAUL McCARTNEY

Moderately fast Rock

BLACKBIRD

CELLO

Words and Music by JOHN LENNON
and PAUL McCARTNEY

CAN'T BUY ME LOVE

Words and Music by JOHN LENNON
and PAUL McCARTNEY

CELLO

COME TOGETHER

CELLO

Words and Music by JOHN LENNON
and PAUL McCARTNEY

Slowly

A DAY IN THE LIFE

CELLO

Words and Music by JOHN LENNON
and PAUL McCARTNEY

DAY TRIPPER

CELLO

Words and Music by JOHN LENNON
and PAUL McCARTNEY

DEAR PRUDENCE

CELLO

Words and Music by JOHN LENNON
and PAUL McCARTNEY

DO YOU WANT TO KNOW A SECRET?

CELLO

Words and Music by JOHN LENNON
and PAUL McCARTNEY

DRIVE MY CAR

Words and Music by JOHN LENNON
and PAUL McCARTNEY

CELLO

EIGHT DAYS A WEEK

CELLO

Words and Music by JOHN LENNON
and PAUL McCARTNEY

ELEANOR RIGBY

CELLO

Words and Music by JOHN LENNON
and PAUL McCARTNEY

Moderately

EVERY LITTLE THING

CELLO

Words and Music by JOHN LENNON
and PAUL McCARTNEY

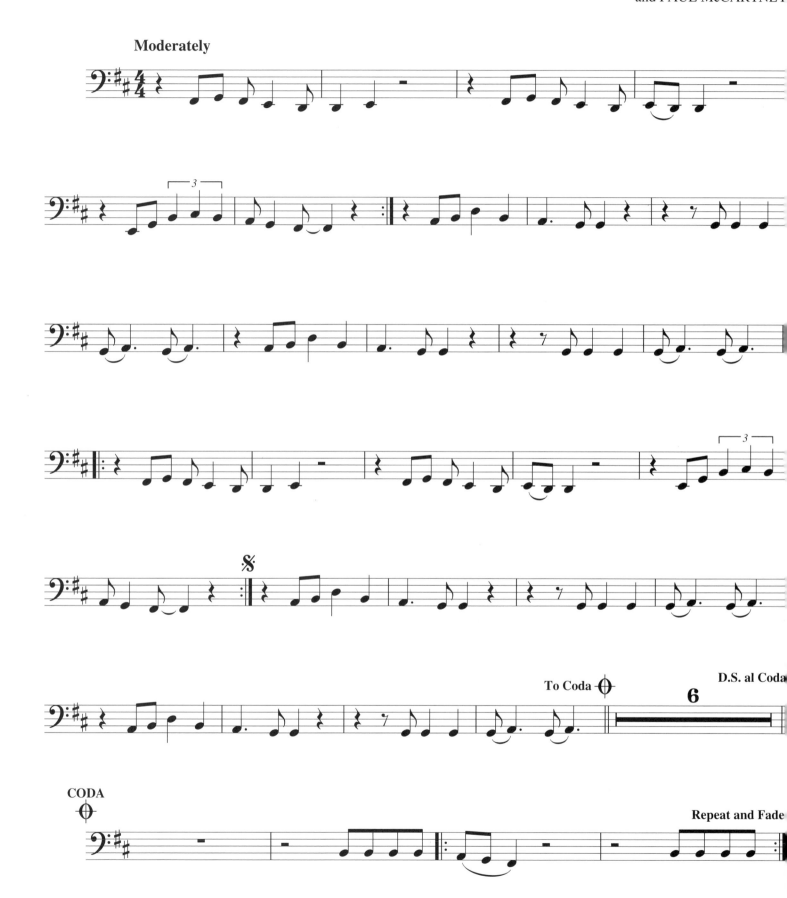

THE FOOL ON THE HILL

Cello

Words and Music by JOHN LENNON
and PAUL McCARTNEY

FROM ME TO YOU

CELLO

Words and Music by JOHN LENNON
and PAUL McCARTNEY

GET BACK

CELLO

Words and Music by JOHN LENNON
and PAUL McCARTNEY

GIRL

CELLO

Words and Music by JOHN LENNON
and PAUL McCARTNEY

GOLDEN SLUMBERS

CELLO

Words and Music by JOHN LENNON
and PAUL McCARTNEY

Moderately

GOOD DAY SUNSHINE

CELLO

Words and Music by JOHN LENNON
and PAUL McCARTNEY

GOT TO GET YOU INTO MY LIFE

CELLO

Words and Music by JOHN LENNON
and PAUL McCARTNEY

A HARD DAY'S NIGHT

CELLO

Words and Music by JOHN LENNON
and PAUL McCARTNEY

HELLO, GOODBYE

CELLO

Words and Music by JOHN LENNON
and PAUL McCARTNEY

Moderately

HELP!

Cello

Words and Music by JOHN LENNON
and PAUL McCARTNEY

HELTER SKELTER

CELLO

Words and Music by JOHN LENNON
and PAUL McCARTNEY

HERE COMES THE SUN

CELLO

Words and Music by
GEORGE HARRISON

HERE, THERE AND EVERYWHERE

Cello

Words and Music by JOHN LENNON
and PAUL McCARTNEY

Moderately slow

HEY JUDE

CELLO

Words and Music by JOHN LENNON
and PAUL McCARTNEY

Slowly

I FEEL FINE

Cello

Words and Music by JOHN LENNON
and PAUL McCARTNEY

I AM THE WALRUS

CELLO

Words and Music by JOHN LENNON
and PAUL McCARTNEY

Slowly

I SAW HER STANDING THERE

CELLO

Words and Music by JOHN LENNON
and PAUL McCARTNEY

Moderately bright, with a beat

I SHOULD HAVE KNOWN BETTER

CELLO

Words and Music by JOHN LENNON
and PAUL McCARTNEY

I WANT TO HOLD YOUR HAND

CELLO

Words and Music by JOHN LENNON
and PAUL McCARTNEY

Moderately

I WILL

CELLO

Words and Music by JOHN LENNON
and PAUL McCARTNEY

I'LL CRY INSTEAD

CELLO

Words and Music by JOHN LENNON
and PAUL McCARTNEY

Brightly

I'LL FOLLOW THE SUN

CELLO

Words and Music by JOHN LENNON
and PAUL McCARTNEY

Moderately

I'M A LOSER

CELLO

Words and Music by JOHN LENNON
and PAUL McCARTNEY

Moderately

I'M HAPPY JUST TO DANCE WITH YOU

CELLO

Words and Music by JOHN LENNON
and PAUL McCARTNEY

I'VE JUST SEEN A FACE

Words and Music by JOHN LENNON
and PAUL McCARTNEY

CELLO

IF I FELL

CELLO

Words and Music by JOHN LENNON
and PAUL McCARTNEY

IN MY LIFE

CELLO

Words and Music by JOHN LENNON
and PAUL McCARTNEY

IT WON'T BE LONG

CELLO

Words and Music by JOHN LENNON
and PAUL McCARTNEY

IT'S ONLY LOVE

CELLO

Words and Music by JOHN LENNON
and PAUL McCARTNEY

Moderately

JULIA

CELLO

Words and Music by JOHN LENNON
and PAUL McCARTNEY

LADY MADONNA

CELLO

Words and Music by JOHN LENNON
and PAUL McCARTNEY

Brightly

LET IT BE

CELLO

Words and Music by JOHN LENNON
and PAUL McCARTNEY

THE LONG AND WINDING ROAD

Cello

Words and Music by JOHN LENNON
and PAUL McCARTNEY

LOVE ME DO

CELLO

Words and Music by JOHN LENNON
and PAUL McCARTNEY

LUCY IN THE SKY WITH DIAMONDS

CELLO

Words and Music by JOHN LENNON
and PAUL McCARTNEY

MAGICAL MYSTERY TOUR

CELLO

Words and Music by JOHN LENNON
and PAUL McCARTNEY

MARTHA MY DEAR

CELLO

Words and Music by JOHN LENNON
and PAUL McCARTNEY

MICHELLE

CELLO

Words and Music by JOHN LENNON
and PAUL McCARTNEY

NO REPLY

CELLO

Words and Music by JOHN LENNON
and PAUL McCARTNEY

NORWEGIAN WOOD

(This Bird Has Flown)

CELLO

Words and Music by JOHN LENNON
and PAUL McCARTNEY

NOWHERE MAN

Cello

Words and Music by JOHN LENNON
and PAUL McCARTNEY

OB-LA-DI, OB-LA-DA

CELLO

Words and Music by JOHN LENNON
and PAUL McCARTNEY

OCTOPUS'S GARDEN

CELLO

Words and Music by RICHARD STARKEY,
JOHN LENNON and PAUL McCARTNEY

Moderately bright

PAPERBACK WRITER

Words and Music by JOHN LENNON
and PAUL McCARTNEY

CELLO

Bright Rock

PENNY LANE

CELLO

Words and Music by JOHN LENNON
and PAUL McCARTNEY

PLEASE PLEASE ME

CELLO

Words and Music by JOHN LENNON
and PAUL McCARTNEY

P.S. I LOVE YOU

CELLO

Words and Music by JOHN LENNON
and PAUL McCARTNEY

REVOLUTION

CELLO

Words and Music by JOHN LENNON
and PAUL McCARTNEY

RUN FOR YOUR LIFE

Cello

Words and Music by JOHN LENNON
and PAUL McCARTNEY

SGT. PEPPER'S LONELY HEARTS CLUB BAND

CELLO

Words and Music by JOHN LENNON
and PAUL McCARTNEY

SHE LOVES YOU

CELLO

Words and Music by JOHN LENNON
and PAUL McCARTNEY

Moderately

SHE'S A WOMAN

CELLO

Words and Music by JOHN LENNON
and PAUL McCARTNEY

SOMETHING

CELLO

Words and Music by
GEORGE HARRISON

STRAWBERRY FIELDS FOREVER

CELLO

Words and Music by JOHN LENNON
and PAUL McCARTNEY

TELL ME WHY

CELLO

Words and Music by JOHN LENNON
and PAUL McCARTNEY

THANK YOU GIRL

CELLO

Words and Music by JOHN LENNON
and PAUL McCARTNEY

THINGS WE SAID TODAY

CELLO

Words and Music by JOHN LENNON
and PAUL McCARTNEY

THIS BOY
(Ringo's Theme)

CELLO

Words and Music by JOHN LENNON
and PAUL McCARTNEY

TICKET TO RIDE

CELLO

Words and Music by JOHN LENNON
and PAUL McCARTNEY

TWIST AND SHOUT

CELLO

Words and Music by BERT RUSSELL
and PHIL MEDLEY

WE CAN WORK IT OUT

Words and Music by JOHN LENNON
and PAUL McCARTNEY

CELLO

WHEN I'M SIXTY-FOUR

CELLO

Words and Music by JOHN LENNON
and PAUL McCARTNEY

WHILE MY GUITAR GENTLY WEEPS

CELLO

Words and Music by
GEORGE HARRISON

WITH A LITTLE HELP FROM MY FRIENDS

CELLO

Words and Music by JOHN LENNON
and PAUL McCARTNEY

THE WORD

Cello

Words and Music by JOHN LENNON
and PAUL McCARTNEY

YELLOW SUBMARINE

Words and Music by JOHN LENNON
and PAUL McCARTNEY

YES IT IS

CELLO

Words and Music by JOHN LENNON
and PAUL McCARTNEY

YESTERDAY

Words and Music by JOHN LENNON
and PAUL McCARTNEY

CELLO

YOU CAN'T DO THAT

CELLO

Words and Music by JOHN LENNON
and PAUL McCARTNEY

YOU WON'T SEE ME

CELLO

Words and Music by JOHN LENNON
and PAUL McCARTNEY

Moderately

YOU'RE GOING TO LOSE THAT GIRL

CELLO

Words and Music by JOHN LENNON
and PAUL McCARTNEY

YOU'VE GOT TO HIDE YOUR LOVE AWAY

CELLO

Words and Music by JOHN LENNON
and PAUL McCARTNEY

YOUR MOTHER SHOULD KNOW

CELLO

Words and Music by JOHN LENNON
and PAUL McCARTNEY